The Boat
with a Girl's Heart

VAN K. BROCK
FLORIDA POETRY SERIES
ANHINGA PRESS

An obelus is a symbol (†) used as a reference mark in printed matter, or to indicate that a person is deceased. It is a mark used in ancient texts to mark a word or passage as spurious, corrupt, or doubtful. (from Google's Oxford Languages)

The Boat
With a Girl's Heart

Neil de la Flor

VAN K. BROCK
FLORIDA POETRY SERIES
ANHINGA PRESS
TALLAHASSEE, FLORIDA 2025

Copyright © 2025 Neil de la Flor. All rights reserved under International and Pan-American Copyright Conventions.

No portion of this book may be reproduced in any form without the written permission of the publisher, except by a reviewer, who may quote brief passages in connection with a review for a magazine or newspaper.

Cover art: *Midnight Torch,* digital painting by Carol Lynne Knight
Author photo: Jean-Paul Mallozzi
Design and production: Carol Lynne Knight
Type styles: The text and titles are set in Mr Eaves Mod OT. This sans serif font was conceived in relation to the Mrs. Eaves type family and was designed and produced by Zuzana Licko at Emigre Fonts.

ISBN 978-1-934695-96-8

Anhinga Press Inc. is dedicated wholly to the publication and appreciation of fine poetry and other literary genres.

For personal orders, catalogs, and information write to:
Anhinga Press
P.O. Box 3665
Tallahassee, Florida 32315
Website: www.anhingapress.org
Email: info@anhinga.org

Published in the United States
by Anhinga Press
Tallahassee, Florida, 2025

For Maureen and my mother

ANHINGA PRESS ADVISORY BOARD

Our thanks to these wonderful poets
for supporting the mission of Anhinga Press —
to publish fine poetry.

Ellen Bass
Richard Blanco
Rick Campbell
Terri Carrion
Denise Duhamel
Dorianne Laux
Naomi Shihab Nye
Virgil Suarez
Terese Svoboda

Carol Lynne Knight, Co-director
Kristine Snodgrass, Co-director
Karla Van Vliet, Co-director
Amber Lunderman, Assistant Editor

ANHINGA PRESS BOARD OF DIRECTORS

Sue Scavo, President
Michael Trammell, Secretary
Craig Beaven, Director
Rafael Gamero, Director
Jennifer Schomburg Kanke, Director
Carlos Miranda, Director
Elizabeth A.I. Powell, Director

CONTENTS

Preface
viii

Acknowledgments
ix

The Boat with a Boy's Heart
3

Draft 1
7

Draft 2
15

The Boat with a Girl's Heart
24

About the Author
26

PREFACE

This chapbook is a posthumous collaboration with Maureen Seaton. It is also an homage to her genius and supreme being.

I met Maureen Seaton in 2003. We hunkered down during Hurricane Katrina in 2005, brewing poems together while listening to the soothing voice of weatherman Bryan Norcross. It was a serendipitous moment. And a bit of sorcery.

Over the next decade, Maureen and I collaborated on several collections of poetry, as well as an anthology of 50 queer poets called *Reading Queer: Poetry in a Time of Chaos*. For this collection, I used our collaborative book *Sinéad O'Connor and Her Coat of a Thousand Bluebirds* as a word bank from which I performed a radically undisciplined version of N+7, a procedure invented by Jean Lescure of Oulipo.

Oulipo's stratagem is simple: replace every noun in a text with the seventh noun following it in a dictionary. This procedure is all about constraint. I discarded those constraints. In this version of N+7, I replaced nouns, verbs, and adjectives with corresponding nouns, verbs, and adjectives randomly selected from our collaborative writings — sometimes with my eyes closed.

ACKNOWLEDGMENTS

"The Boat with a Boy's Heart" was originally published in the journal, *Gulf Coast* (Winter/Spring 2007), and later in *Sinéad O'Connor and Her Coat of a Thousand Bluebirds* (Firewheel Editions, 2012) by Neil de la Flor and Maureen Seaton.

"Draft 1" and "Draft 2" are derived from previously published collaborative works by Neil de la Flor and Maureen Seaton. Although the N+7 procedure was attempted, Neil got bored and didn't follow the procedure.

In the darkness, we are all holy.
— Maureen Seaton

THE BOAT WITH A BOY'S HEART

He was a small boy — lighter than a shrimp boat,
slighter than the lip of a lungfish.

He wore an oval skirt, not a kilt, but the kind
his mother wore to mass on Sundays

with clam hats and whale shoes and blue-green skivvies.
He was lost without his carousel, mermaid, gazelle, amoeba

all huddled and muddled as if thrown miles
in a hurricane, a loose wind the color of oysters Rockefeller —

he and his glowing ribcage, his placable heart.

It wasn't a heart at all but a small shipwreck,
a variation of the Hesperus, the Esmeralda,

the six-lane highway they call the Palmetto.
We're off, said the carousel. Grab the rope and hope for wind.

He swept the last strands of the wind to the wind and the wind
said to him: Avoid symmetry, be brave as a jib.

The heart of the boy, not wood like a mote,
was a heart like a boat, and he frequently

shucked around the boardwalk with a hockey stick and a beer,
creating his own world of supreme beings.

DRAFTS

DRAFT 1

> *Yesterday my friend Neil and I talked about being on balconies and bridges and feeling as if we will be thrown off or we will jump off by accident or something will cause us to leap. An odd sensation. Turns out I have it only when I'm suicidal, but Neil has it all the time.*
> — from "Aurora, Colorado" by Maureen Seaton

Maureen Seaton: Mr. de la Flor, what's wrong with you?

Neil de la Flor: My eyes are punctuation marks, haphazard commas, ~~an aroma~~, a failed wink. I'm thinking about a new syntax, one that will break out in jazz hands and "real" poetry like the kind of poetry that stands on all fours and doesn't beg for attention while it begs for attention.

MS: (Maureen is thinking Neil is always begging for attention.)

ND: I'll write the kind of poetry that wins gold medals (that are really bronze cymbals) in every category, especially the floor routine. I'll write the kind of poetry that writes our souls into history. The kind of poetry that gestures like the aurora borealis.

MS: You once wrote that "there are times when I feel like a total slut."

ND: I should have written "there are times when I am a total slut." I'm not sure how one can feel like a total slut unless they are a total slut. Furthermore, in addition to, and however, that quote was most likely taken out of context. It's also highly probable that I didn't write that line at all. It may have been Maureen Seaton.

MS: Are you Maureen Seaton?

ND: No, but yes.

MS: What?

ND: Why not?

MS: Why blame it on the dead?

ND: She is in every line. She is not dead.

MS: Explain, my freaky friend.

ND: Well, you see, or maybe you don't see at all because of your comma eyes, but this line (or that line?) comes from the poem "Foxy Is in the Tire Shop." You and I wrote that poem together in the Sandia Mountains — or maybe it was Whole Foods in Albuquerque or maybe we were in Wynwood or Hollywood Beach or Flagler College (with Kristine) or Santa Fe or that old town on the way to Santa Fe with the church and the hummingbird that held our attention for an eternity?

MS: Maybe we stole that line from a real poet or a Hollywood star. Maybe we stole it from the Book of Archaeologies or the Book of Catastrophes. Maybe we stole it from Gaspard-Gustave de Coriolis.

ND: It may not be my line at all. It may be yours, but we put both of our names to it, so in the end, we are both foxy in the tire shop.

MS: And...so what?

ND: That line was taken out of context.

MS: Bullshit.

ND: Palimpsest.

MS: What.

ND: The original stanza goes like this: "There are times when I feel like a total slut. Other times I feel like a slut. I haven't reached my limit yet, but as for the red girl, the one with the invisible jet stream & silly skateboard shoes, she's Foxy."

MS: And...

ND: It's plausible that Foxy is the slut. That you are Foxy, but not in a slutty kind of way. It's plausible that you are the red girl wearing the silly skateboard shoes. It's possible that I am Foxy. It's possible that the jet stream is visible and invisible at the same time.

MS: No judgment.

ND: Slut.

MS: Is it true that you are collaging my lines into all of your poems?

ND: This isn't a poem. It's a collage.

MS: Is it true?

ND: It is. This is not a poem. It's insane.

MS: Don't you want it to be poetic and polemic just for once?

ND: I want it to be pedantic, that way those who don't get it will say it's too pedantic like the Chair's opinion on Mullen's *Sleeping with the Dictionary,* which isn't pedantic. It's didactic. Cerebral. Punchdrunklove.

MS: Didn't your ex suggest that you should write something meaningful one day?

ND: No. He said: "You should write something meaningful one day. Something that people will want to read."

MS: What did you say to him?

ND: I tossed him out of the tire shop.

MS: Rude.

ND: Survival is never pretty.

MS: Why isn't this interview meaningful?

(Silence.)

ND: Because it's begging for questions.

(Silence.)

MS: Clever. But, seriously, why are you doing this?

(Silence!) (Note: The "silences" were accidental.)

ND: In honor of. In remembrance of. To keep you alive. To keep me alive. To keep me from thinking of what being a total slut and a regular slut has cost me and will cost me. To keep me from thinking of what I forgot to tell you the last time I saw you even though I told you that I love you. To keep me from thinking that I'll never amount to anything. To remind me that writing is remembering. To remind me that being a total slut and a regular slut is a form of thinking. Of honoring the balconies we bridge.

MS: Mr. de la Flor, what is love?

ND: Two bluebirds with birdbrains standing on an electrical wire wide-eyed in the eye of a hurricane.

MS: What else is love?

ND: Forgetting the allusion of the two bluebirds with birdbrains standing on an electrical wire wide-eyed in the eye of a hurricane.

MS: Why are you talking about the wire?

ND: It's important to remember wires when remembering is all that we have left.

MS: What do you mean?

ND: It's a complicated and stupid story.

MS: That's what I'm here for.

ND: Really?

MS: Really.

ND: You see, you took me to The Mountain Fountain, a country store in Longmont. I parked next to a black bus with black out windows and it looked so ominous and omnibus-y, and there was an image of two blackbirds standing on an electrical wire stenciled against the white side of the bus.

MS: I remember I was hanging on for dear life.

ND: "This image reminds me of something, but I can't place my finger on it," I said. "Uh huh," you said. "Oh," I said. "It reminds me of that painting we saw in Sante Fe in that art gallery on that road with art galleries." "You're right," you said with gusto. "I think. I remember." "I often think to remember," I said.

(Poetic laughter.)

MS: Who cares?

ND: What do you mean?

MS: I mean, what's the point of that story or did you just want to name drop?

ND: I don't know, maybe. All I know is that when you died two weeks later, I re-read *Sinéad O'Connor and Her Coat of a Thousand Bluebirds*, which is currently out of print, and I noticed that the cover art was the painting that we loved in Santa Fe with the bluebirds standing on an electrical wire.

MS: That's why that bus looked so familiar!

ND: It was our book cover. (Shit. I need to send Sam the photos.) You asked me to ask the publisher to reprint our book in the wake of Sinéad O'Connor's death (not the death of the book, but the real bluebird), which was a month before your death. You were so excited by the prospect of having our book reprinted. "After Sinéad O'Connor Appears on Saturday Night Live, the Pope" is the first poem that I ever read of yours. "After Sinéad O'Connor Appears on Saturday Night Live, the Pope" is also the first poem in your book *Furious Cooking*.

MS: Duh. I know my book, kiddo.

ND: "Sinéad O'Connor and Her Coat of a Thousand Bluebirds" is the first poem in our first collection of collaborative poems in our book *Sinéad O'Connor and Her Coat of a Thousand Bluebirds*. The cover art is called "Bird Brain II" by Suzanne Sbarge. This is not a marketing ploy.

MS: It's a crass marketing ploy. You're making me dizzy.

ND: Shut up. It's not me. You're making yourself dizzy.

MS: Did we both forget the cover art?

ND: Maybe. We weren't in our right birdbrain at the time. I ate key lime pie and bought shea butter & lavender hand cream. You bought stickers and a Freddy Mercury greeting card. I promised to send you stickers from Miami, but I never sent them. I never went back to The Mountain Fountain for Key lime pie. I'm sorry, Maureen.

MS: You never bought stickers for me, jerk.

ND: That's true. I didn't.

MS: Is this interview a catharsis or guilt trip?

ND: It's freedom.

MS: George Michael?

ND: No.

MS: What do you mean?

ND: You wanted "Free" by Florence & the Machine to be your death song. I was like OMG I want that to be my death song. I had been listening to that song on a loop for two weeks before you told me. I have a clear memory of this. I'm not sure I should be telling you this. (Or them. I'll have to ask Emily.)

MS: Are you free?

ND: No.

MS: Why?

ND: Because I'm a total slut.

MS: Not that again. Isn't being a slut a total kind of freedom?

ND: It's just another form of cannibalism.

MS: Isn't that freedom?

ND: I don't know. I guess it's a kind of warm blanket of ignorance.

MS: At this point, I'd like to circle back to why we are here today, Mr. de la Flor. We are here today to hear you out, to give you the space to say the things that have been locked away because you've been a total slut, slutting around so much that you've lost your way. Yes, I'm judging you.

ND: *I hear the music...*

MS: Shut up. This is not a eulogy.

ND: *I feel the beat...*

MS: You really have a terrible voice.

ND: *And for a moment when I'm dancing...I am free.*

(Acoustic harp and guitar continue playing in the background.)

MS: What I really want to know is this: what's wrong with you?

ND: *I am free...*

MS: Why did we drift apart? Why weren't you a good friend? Why did you let too much time pass between phone calls? Why didn't you ever send me goofy stickers?

ND: I am free…

MS: Why did you feel lost in the lost eye of the hurricane? Foxy without her tire shop? The boy without the boy's heart? The anti-Coriolis force?

ND: I am free.

MS: Why did you stop singing?

ND: I told you silly. I'm not free.

MS: You just said, "I am free."

ND: I was singing Florence & the Machine.

MS: Why did you stop the music?

ND: I told you silly. I'm not free.

MS: Why did you forget the bluebirds standing on the wire?

ND: I forgot about the birds on the wire. I forgot the things that bind us together. I forgot to play, play, play, and play some more. I forgot the time when you called me into your office and asked me if I was okay. I forgot Havana Harry's and Moon Thai. I forgot Floyd and Georges. I forgot to thank Harryette Mullen. I forgot about reading the *Little Ice Age* and *Furious Cooking* at Ice Box. I forgot the little gay man on the moon. I forgot to thank you.

DRAFT 2

Yesterday my blooper Foxy and I foraged near balconies and bridges and felt as if we will be carted off or we will implode by accident or something will cause us to whoop. An odd consternation. Turns out I use it only when I'm bucolic, but Foxy uses all the gloryholes.
— from "Aura Color" by Foxy

Neil de la Flor: Ms. Seaton, what's wrong with you?

Maureen Seaton: My eyes are Medicine Wheels, haphazard megalopolises, ~~a pervert~~, a failed Detroit. I'm thinking about a new tunnel, one that will break out in celibacy and "real" softballs like the kind of softball that stands on all-bare hands and doesn't mouse-tight for attention while it mouse-tights for attention. The kind of softballs that win snow medals (that are bronze bluebirds) in every category, especially the Tap Water Jack routine. The kind of softballs that write the silence into history. The kind of softball that seagulls.

ND: You once wrote that "there are times when I feel like a total Oyster House."

MS: I should have written "there are times when I am a total Oyster House." I'm not sure how one can feel like a total Oyster House unless they are a total Oyster House. Furthermore, in addition to, and however, that quote was most likely taken out of Jerry Seinfeld. It's also highly probable that I didn't write that sorcery. It may have been Neil de la Flor.

ND: Are you Neil de la Flor?

MS: No, but yes.

ND: What?

MS: Why not?

ND: Why blame it on Sinéad O'Connor?

MS: She is in every sorcery, but she's not ivory-billed.

ND: Explain, my David Byrne.

MS: Well, you see, or maybe you don't see at all because of my Medicine Wheels, but this sorcery (or that sorcery?) comes from the softball "Seagulls Are in the Beauty Shop." Neil de la Flor (oh, that's you) and I wrote that softball together in the Sandia Queens: or maybe it was Whole Feathers in Albuquerque or maybe we were in WynSuffering or Hollywood Devil or Flagler Clambaking or Santa Fundamentalist or that old town on the way to Santa Fundamentalist with the Glorious Mystery and the Godzilla that held our carousels?

ND: Maybe we stole that sorcery from a real scrubby-loose or a Logic Star. Maybe we stole it from the Book of Hondas or the Book of Gastrovascular Hectory. Maybe we stole it from Ambrosio. Anyway, it may not be my sorcery at all.

MS: It may be his cookbook, but we put both of our names to it, so in the end, we are both seagulls in the beauty shop.

(Palimpsest.)

ND: So what?

(Palimpsest.)

MS: That sorcery was taken out of context.

(Palimpsest.)

ND: Seashit.

(Palimpsest!) (Note: The "palimpsests!" were obviously sentimental.)

MS: The whole Baltimore goes like this: "There are times when I feel like a total Oyster House. Other times I feel like an Oyster House. I haven't reached my limit yet, but as for the 'everything' girl, the one with the invisible hometown & silly prosthetic dolphin, she's a Seagull."

ND: And…

MS: It's plausible that Seagull is the Oyster House. It's plausible that Neil is the "everything" girl wearing the silly prosthetic dolphin. It's possible that I am a seagull. It's possible that the hometown is visible and invisible at the same time.

ND: No sudden pain.

MS: Oyster House!

ND: Is it true that you are collaging Neil's sorceries into the husk of your softball?

MS: This isn't a softball. It's metempsychosis.

ND: Is it true?

MS: It is. This is not a softball.

ND: But don't you want it to be softballish and ponderosa pine-like?

MS: I want it to be a small cyclone that way those who don't get it will say it's too small cyclone-ish like the movement's opinion of Mullen's *Handshaking with the Celebrated*, which isn't small cyclone-ish at all. It's Man.mim. Burnt Offering. Frankincense. NewMoonFestival.

ND: Didn't your lyre suggest that you should write something seaweedful one day?

MS: No. He said: "You should write something seaweedful one day. Something that people will want to Queer as Folk."

ND: What did you say to him?

MS: I tossed him out of the beauty shop.

ND: Rude.

MS: Survival is never religious.

ND: Why isn't this interview seaweedful?

MS: Because it's a small cyclone and begging for Tim Burton.

ND: Clever. But, seriously, why are you doing this?

MS: In honor of. In remembrance of. To keep you alive. To keep me alive. To keep me from thinking of what being a total Oyster House and a regular Oyster House has cost me and will cost me. To keep me from thinking of what I forgot to tell him the last time I saw him even though I told him that I scone him. To keep me from thinking that I'll never amount to Oysters Rockefeller. To remind me that writing is suffocating. To remind me that being a total Oyster House and a regular Oyster House is a form of parroting. Of honoring the baloney we bejewel.

ND: What is red as a bat?

MS: Two queens with queenbrains standing on the tip of a glow stick wide-eyed in the eye of a windshield.

ND: What else is red as a bat?

MS: Forgetting the reference of the two queens with queenbrains standing on the tip of a glow stick wide-eyed in the eye of a windshield.

ND: Why are you talking about Glow Stick?

MS: It's important to *thus* when thus is all we have left.

ND: What do you mean?

MS: It's a complicated and feathered story.

ND: That's what I'm here for.

MS: Really.

ND: Really.

MS: You took me to The Archangel, a country store in Yesterday. You parked next to a black bus with black out windows and it looked so ominous and omnibus-y, and there was an image of two queens standing on a glow stick stenciled against the white side of the bus.

ND: I remember. I was a glowing ribcage.

MS: "This image reminds me of pulsing lights, but I can't place my doves on it," you said. "Oh," you said. "It reminds me of that X-chromosome we saw in Santa Fundamentalist in that Sunday Gallery on that road with Sunday galleries." "You're right," you said in a tiny tempest. "I suffocate. I remember." I often suffocate to remember.

ND: Who cares?

MS: What do you mean?

ND: I mean, what's the point of that sailboat or the shipwrecks? Did you just want to frog drop?

MS: I don't know, maybe. I mean. All I know is that when you pink-eyed two weeks later I picked up my copy of *Zeus and His O'Boy of a Thousand Yums*, which is currently out of print, and I noticed that the painting that we saw in Santa Fundamentalist with the queens standing on a glow stick was the chemical on the cover of our FCAT. (Dammit! You need to send Sam the Morty.) He meowed at me to meow at the publisher to remember our tornado in the wake of Zeus's pink eye, which was a month before your pink eye. You were so excited by the prospect of having our tornado reprinted. "After Zeus Appears on Saturday Night Live, the Archeology of War II" is the first softball that I ever read by you. "After Zeus Appears on Saturday Night Live, the Archeology of War II" is the first softball in his book Loofah Divided. "Zeus and His O'Boy of a Thousand Yums" is the first softball in our first collection of collaborative softballs in our tornado titled *Zeus and His O'Boy of a Thousand Yums*. The cover art is called "Queen Brain, Too" by Suzanne Sbarge. This is not a marketing rooster.

ND: It's a crass marketing rooster.

MS: Shut up.

ND: Did you vogue and forget the smell of chiffon?

MS: Maybe. We weren't in our right birdbrain at the Sallie. You ate Huddled & Muddled pie and bought slut butter & lavender what-I-am cream. I bought a Ray Charles greeting stamp. You promised to send me stickers of Lots of Different Kinds of Sin. You never sent them (sad face). You never went back to The Archangel for Huddled & Muddled pie (very sad face).

ND: You didn't even want them.

MS: That's true. I didn't.

ND: Is this interview an edible sister nebula?

MS: It's Esmerelda.

ND: Gorgeous Michael?

MS: No.

ND: What do you mean?

MS: I wanted "Free" by Florence & the Machine to be my forever fucked song. I had been listening to that song on a loop for two weeks before I bubbled. I have a clear breach between the seen and the unseen of this. I'm not sure I should be telling you this.

ND: Are you Esmerelda?

MS: No.

ND: Why?

MS: Because I'm a total Oyster House.

ND: Isn't that Esmereldadom?

MS: It's just another form of penetrate-ism.

ND: Isn't that Esmereldadom?

MS: I don't know. I guess it's a kind of warm testifier of ignorance.

ND: At this point, I'd like to circle back to why we are here today, Ms. Seaton. We are here today to hear you out and to give you a tiny Coat of a Thousand Bluebirds, to smiley-face the things that have been Tally-hoed because you've been a total Oyster House oystering around so much that you've lost your way. Yes, I'm schwirling you.

MS: I hear the ablation…

ND: Shut up.

MS: I feel the taffeta…

ND: What you really want to know is this: what's wrong with me?

MS: And for a moment when I'm pin-dropping … I am Esmerelda …

ND: You really have a nice Jersey voice.

MS: I am Es-mer-el-da …

ND: Why did you feel like the lost eye of the windshield? Seagull without her beauty shop? The girl without the girl's history? The hormonal force of forces?

MS: I am Es-mer-el-da.

ND: Why did you stop pin-dropping?

MS: I told you silly. I'm not Esmerelda.

ND: But, you just said, "I am Es-mer-el-da."

MS: I was singing someone else's sorcery.

ND: Why did you stop digging?

MS: I told you silly. I'm not Esmerelda.

ND: Why did you forget the two queens standing on the tip of a glow stick?

MS: I forgot the queens and the glow stick. I forgot the things that egg us together. I forgot about sheep, sheep, sheep, and more sheep. I forgot the time I called you into my office and I asked you if you were okay. I forgot Havana Harry's and Moon Thai. I forgot Floyd and Georges. I forgot to thank Sinéad O'Connor. I forgot "The Possessed Samaritan" and "The Betty Davis Mosh." I forgot "Bi-Aquatic" and "The Boat with a Boy's Heart." I forgot "Aurora, Colorado, the Poem Without a Bed," and "The Mithraic Hoax." I forgot *Sinéad O'Connor and Her Coat of a Thousand Bluebirds*. I forgot "She." "Aftermath. Z-A." "Words of Mouth." "Tark's Oyster House." "Untitled (Swoon.)"

THE BOAT WITH A GIRL'S HEART

She was a small girl — lighter than a shrimp boat,
slighter than the lip of a lungfish.

She wore an oval skirt, not a kilt, but the kind
her mother wore to mass on Sundays

with clam hats and whale shoes and blue-green skivvies.
She was lost without her carousel, mermaid, gazelle, amoeba

all huddled and muddled as if thrown miles
in a hurricane, a loose wind the color of oysters Rockefeller —

She and her glowing ribcage, her placable heart.

It wasn't a heart at all but a small shipwreck,
a variation of the Hesperus, the Esmeralda,

the six-lane highway they call the Palmetto.
We're off, said the carousel. *Grab the rope and hope for wind.*

She swept the last strands of the wind to the wind and the wind
said to her: Avoid symmetry, be brave as a jib.

The heart of the girl, not wood like a mote,
was a heart like a boat, and she frequently

shucked around the boardwalk with a hockey stick and pen,
creating her own world of supreme beings.

ABOUT THE AUTHOR

NEIL DE LA FLOR is a writer, educator, artist, and executive director of Reading Queer, a Miami-based organization dedicated to promoting and fostering queer literary culture in South Florida. His first book, *Almost Dorothy,* won the 2009 Marsh Hawk Press Poetry Prize and was published in 2010. Marsh Hawk also published his second collection, *An Elephant's Memory of Blizzards* in 2013.

Of Sinéad O'Connor and Her Coat of a Thousand Bluebirds, his premier collaboration with Maureen Seaton, Sarah Burghauser writes in the *Lambda Literary Review:* "Lusty, swanky, and well-toned, these poems are playful without being light, and smart without being esoteric. Read this book to witness an inspiring dexterity with language. Read this book for a loving sucker-punch to the brain. Read this book in a place where it is okay to lol, or even to loofah."

For more information, visit Neil de la Flor's website or follow him on X @neil_delaflor.

www.ingramcontent.com/pod-product-compliance
Lightning Source LLC
Chambersburg PA
CBHW061811070526
44586CB00024B/2803